Unique Places

Judith Harper

sundance
A Haights Cross Communications Company

Published by
Sundance Publishing
P.O. Box 740
One Beeman Road
Northborough, MA 01532–0740
800-343-8204
www.sundancepub.com

Unique Places
ISBN 0-7608-9635-6

Illustrations by Matt Phillips; pp. 20–21 by Jane Shasky

Photo Credits:
Cover (background map) ©Royalty-Free/CORBIS, ©Hubert Stadler/CORBIS;
p. 1 ©Earl & Nazima Kowall/CORBIS; p. 6 (top) Siegfried Layda/Getty Images,
(bottom) ©Catherine Karnow/CORBIS; p. 7 (top) ©Pierre Vauthey/CORBIS
SYGMA, (bottom) Ernst Haas/Getty Images; p. 8 (background) ©Hrafnsson
Gisli Egill/CORBIS SYGMA, (left) ©CORBIS, (right) Krafft/Photo Researchers, Inc.;
p. 9 ©Paul A. Souders/CORBIS; p. 10 (left) ©Royalty-Free/CORBIS, (right)
©Richard T. Nowitz/CORBIS; p. 11 Anders Geidemark/Getty Images; p. 14 (top)
©The Mariners' Museum/CORBIS, (bottom) ©Royalty-Free/CORBIS; p. 15 (top)
©Martin Harvey/Gallo Images/CORBIS, (right) ©Bruce Coleman Inc./Alamy;
p. 16 (left) Nick Caloyianis/National Geographic/Getty Images; p. 17 (top)
©Wolfgang Kaehler/CORBIS; p. 18 Harbor Branch Oceanographic Institution/
California Academy of Sciences (HBOI/CAS); p. 19 (top) April Goldfinch,
Smithsonian National Museum of Natural History, (center) Dave Pawson,
Smithsonian National Museum of Natural History, (bottom) John E. McCosker,
HBOI/CAS; p. 24 ©Royalty-Free/CORBIS; p. 25 (top) ©Jacques Langevin/CORBIS
SYGMA, (bottom) courtesy of the International Snow Leopard Trust; p. 27
(top) ©De Agostini/The Natural History Museum Picture Library, London,
(bottom) Keystone/Getty Images; p. 28 Roy Toft/National Geographic/Getty
Images; p. 29 (top) David Edwards/National Geographic/Getty Images,
(bottom) ©Earl & Nazima Kowall/CORBIS

Printed in Canada

Table of Contents

Iceland

Brrrr! Iceland! The country with the name that can make you shiver is not as cold and icy as it sounds.

Iceland is the second largest island in the North Atlantic Ocean. Huge sheets of ice, or **glaciers**, cover about one-eighth of the entire land. Some of these ice sheets are more than 3,000 feet thick— that's the height of a small mountain! But to heat things up, Iceland also has earthquakes, hot springs, and fiery volcanoes!

Because the human population of Iceland is small, the island offers unspoiled places where animals like the Arctic fox can live. And many types of sea birds, marine mammals, and fish are able to thrive along Iceland's coastline.

Let's find out more as we explore this land of ice and fire.

Where Fire Meets Ice

Iceland's surface is constantly changing because active volcanoes continue to erupt beneath huge, icy glaciers.

Strokkur Geyser

An Underground Heating System

Iceland's heat is all under its glaciers and ground. All year round, near-boiling water spurts up from under the earth, creating world-famous hot springs and **geysers**. But how does the water get so hot? **Magma**—the hot, liquid rock from volcanoes underneath the earth's surface—heats the underground water.

If you and your family lived in Iceland, you'd never have to worry about expensive heating bills! Icelanders use the abundance of underground hot water to heat their houses, schools, and workplaces. Icelanders also love to swim in naturally heated outdoor pools, especially in the winter.

A group of girls cover their faces in foam from a naturally heated pool near Reykjavik, Iceland.

Surtsey: A Fiery Island Is Born

Let's find out how one Icelandic island appeared about 40 years ago. Back in November 1963, there was only ocean where Surtsey now sits. Then, on November 8, an underwater volcano erupted. Tons of red-hot lava shot high into the air like a giant fountain. A week later, an island of **lava** appeared. For the next three and a half years, the lava kept flowing. Gradually the island cooled. Plants began to grow, and eventually animals arrived. Today seals and seabirds rest on Surtsey's moss-covered rocks.

Surtsey's rocky surface

Here is a look at the erupting volcano that created Surtsey Island.

SOME MAJOR VOLCANIC ERUPTIONS

2004

A volcano in southeastern Iceland erupts. Thick clouds of ash drift toward Europe.

The same volcano that erupts in 2004 erupts and causes a huge flood by melting part of a glacier.

1996

1973

1963–1967

A volcano on the island of Heimaey erupts. All residents are evacuated. The lava adds one square mile of land to the island.

The island of Surtsey is created during a continuous eruption.

Iceland's worst disaster occurs when Mount Laki erupts. About 9,000 people die of starvation because dense clouds of smoke and ash cause crops to fail.

1783–1794

Mount Heckla erupts for the first time. It has erupted many times since then, most recently in 2000.

1104

Iceland Lives Up to Its Name

You would find icy glaciers, chilly ocean waters, and cold winds if you visit Iceland. But many animals thrive there, in spite of these conditions. Let's take a look.

A Huge Sheet of Ice

Visitors to Iceland can take a tour that lets them ride around on top of the third-largest glacier in the world. It's an ice sheet that covers more than 3,000 square miles. That's more than twice the size of the state of Rhode Island. Much of this glacier is thicker than half a mile. It looks quiet from the surface, but volcanoes lie underneath all of the ice.

One of these volcanoes erupted in 1996. Lava and steam poured out and up to meet the glacier. This made the ice melt very fast—too fast—and caused an enormous flood. A huge wall of water that was like a tidal wave destroyed the only bridge that connected eastern Iceland and western Iceland. But because so few people live in this area, no one was hurt.

Moss campion flowers grow above a glacier.

Riches of the Sea

Are you interested in wildlife? Then the coast of Iceland is the place to be! In all seasons, millions of shorebirds, sea mammals, and fish find plenty of food in the sea. More than eight million puffins raise their families on Iceland's rocky cliffs. That's as many puffins as there are people living in New York City— our most populated city!

A baby puffin perches on a young girl's head while she holds three more in her arm.

Atlantic puffins

WHO WILL SAVE THE PUFFLINGS?

Every August, the puffins fly away from the island of Heimaey. Making their first flight from the cliffs at night, some baby puffins, or pufflings, get confused. They fly into town and crash land. But the children of the island gently put the pufflings in boxes, which they take to the shore the next day. The children hold the birds in their hands and toss them into the air. The pufflings then fly off to join the other puffins!

Eastern Atlantic harbor seals like this one swallow their food whole or in chunks rather than chew it.

Thousands of harbor seals also live along the coastline, but Iceland can be a dangerous place for these seals. That's because Icelanders continue to hunt them. An adult seal eats at least ten pounds of fish every day, and many Icelanders believe that the seals' appetite harms their valuable fishing industry. Iceland harvests more than two million tons of fish each year. That's enough for 8 billion human-size fish dinners!

Quit hogging all the fish!

The Galapagos Islands

You are now entering an animal paradise. Where in the world are you? You're in the Pacific Ocean on the equator. To be exact, you are 600 miles west of the South American country of Ecuador.

As you walk on these sun-warmed islands, be careful where you step! The dark rocks by the sea are covered with lizards. Climb over the rocks toward the sea. The blue-green ocean waters are full of life.

Because the Galapagos Islands are so far away from other land masses, they are home to animals and plants found nowhere else in the world. Bird sounds fill the air, and even the land itself is alive. When active volcanoes erupt, the lava flows freely.

Reptile Heaven

Both land and sea lizards cling to the islands' rocks. And giant turtles called tortoises can be found on many islands. The Spanish named the island Galapagos because it is their word for tortoise.

Sailors capture giant tortoises.

Tortoises—Galapagos Giants

What's six feet long and can weigh up to 600 pounds? Why, a Galapagos giant tortoise, of course. About 10,000-15,000 of these giant tortoises live on the islands. Hundreds of years ago, there were 250,000 of them. But over the years, people, including sailors, captured and killed them for their meat.

Galapagos giant tortoise

The ploughshare tortoise is one of the rarest land tortoises in the world. It is named for the plough-shaped piece of shell between its front legs.

Manchineel leaves

The tortoises often live to be well over 100 years old. Some reach a ripe old age of 150 years or more! They are plant eaters, and munch on cactus and the leaves from the **manchineel** tree. Oddly enough, the fruit of this tree is poisonous to most animals, including humans, so there are plenty of leaves for the tortoises.

 ## WHAT'S THE OLDEST ANIMAL ON EARTH?

Do you think you'd ever get tired of having a birthday? You might if you were Harriet. After all, she's had 174 of them! Harriet is a Galapagos tortoise who lives in a zoo in Australia. Scientists say that she was born around 1830. That's 31 years before the Civil War! She now lives in a zoo in Australia.

Marine iguana underwater

Lizards by the Sea

Marine iguanas are lizards that spend time on both land and sea. They love the sun, so the warm lava rocks by the sea make perfect iguana resting spots. If the iguanas are hot or hungry, they dive in the water. Sometimes they stay underwater for as long as an hour. When they get thirsty, they drink seawater, but the iguanas need to snort the salt out of their bodies. All it takes is a few good sneezes, and salt crystals come out of their nostrils.

Marine iguanas spend a lot of time sunning themselves on rocks by the shore.

A land iguana munches on a prickly-pear cactus.

Land iguanas only live on land, not in the sea. These colorful yellow and orange animals creep over rocks and sand. Their strong muscles and claws help them climb trees so that they can munch on leaves and fruit. Their favorite meal is cactus, especially the prickly-pear cactus.

Cannonball!

Prickly-pear cactus in bloom

An Ocean Wonderland

Because the Galapagos Islands are full of unique animals and plants, people come from all over the world to see them. Some people just want to scuba dive and look around. Others come to study and learn.

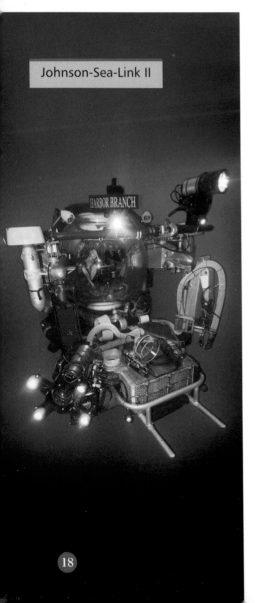

Johnson-Sea-Link II

HARBOR BRANCH

Scientific Exploration

Scientists travel to the Galapagos Islands often. Dr. Carole Baldwin, a fish expert, went there in 1998 and took many trips in an underwater vehicle called the Johnson-Sea-Link II.

This underwater vessel is perfect for studying and collecting sea creatures. It has a robotic arm that reaches out and grabs the animals that the scientists want to study, and it can go as deep as 3,000 feet. That's thousands of feet deeper than a human can scuba dive. The Galapagos exploration trips were magical, Dr. Baldwin says. She and her team discovered many unknown **species** of animals in the deep waters!

New Galapagos Animals

What new creatures did the team find? They discovered a new kind of shark. This small green-eyed fish belongs to the family of catsharks. The team also found a new species of pencil urchin. And these are just a few of the new species found by just one team. Who knows how many other unique plants and animals are still to be discovered in the waters around the Galapagos?

This pencil urchin scrapes tiny creatures from rocks with its sharp teeth.

A new species of sun star

This new species of catshark is about 1.5 feet long.

LIFE ON THE GALAPAGOS ISLANDS

How did many of the more common plants and animals of the Galapagos Islands get there? Here's what some scientists think!

Birds may have carried seeds from other places or left them in the soil after digesting the seeds.

We know that whaling ships in the 19th century carried rats that made it to the islands. Crews also left goats and pigs there. They planned to use them for food when they returned.

Pieces of driftwood may have carried land animals including tortoises, iguanas, and insects to the islands.

The Galapagos

600 miles

SOUTH AMERICA

We know that settlers have brought cattle to the island from South America.

Grasses and loose seeds shaken free by the wind may have blown onto the islands from South America.

Sea lions and Galapagos penguins may have swum to the islands.

21

Mongolia

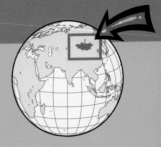

Welcome to Mongolia—a land that has millions of animals, but few people! The best way to see this country is the way Mongolians have for thousands of years— on horseback.

If you could gallop on a horse across the vast grasslands, you'd find Mongolian herders raising sheep, goats, horses, and cattle. Guiding your horse up the rugged mountains and through the thick forests, you'd probably find wild animals—wolves, wild sheep, the rare musk deer, and the **endangered** snow leopard.

Traveling south to the Gobi Desert, you would trade your horse for a two-humped camel. As you went, you would keep your eye out for dinosaur bones. Eighty million years ago, this desert was a top dinosaur hang-out!

Saving the Snow Leopard

Hear that loud purring noise? It's not coming from your average kitty. This big cat prowls the mountains of Mongolia. These leopards are in danger, and the Mongolians are trying to save them.

The Herders vs. the Snow Leopards

Snow leopards have never had an easy life, but it's getting tougher. Scientists believe there are only 4,500–7,500 of these cats left in the entire world. About 1,000 of them are trying to survive in Mongolia.

THE SNOW LEOPARD

A 3-foot-long tail helps the leopard keep its balance on steep cliffs. It also wraps around the animal on cold winter nights.

It stands 2 feet at the shoulder—the same height as a German shepherd.

Short, sturdy forelegs and longer, powerful hindlegs make the leopard sure-footed.

A long outer coat and a thick, woolly undercoat protect the leopard from sub-zero cold.

So what's the problem? More Mongolians have become herders. These new herders need land to graze their sheep and goats. The problem is that the grazing land is close to the snow leopard's **habitat**. And the herders have pushed out or killed the snow leopard's prey. So what do the hungry snow leopards do? To survive, they kill the herders' animals. Then the herders kill the snow leopards to protect their sheep and goats.

A Mongolian boy on a pony holds a kid goat.

Its fur color ranges from off-white to smoky gray with black spots. This coloring helps leopards to hunt and to hide from humans.

The paws act like snowshoes, which prevent sinking into the snow.

SAVE A SNOW LEOPARD!

Is there a way to protect the snow leopard? That's what wildlife workers are hoping. Their plan is to help the herders. Because the herders are poor, the wildlife workers help them sell their crafts around the world. In return, the herders promise not to kill the snow leopard. And here's the good news! So far the plan is working because more snow leopards in Mongolia are surviving.

Mongolian finger puppets

25

The Gobi Desert's Secrets

Mongolia's Gobi Desert is a goldmine—for people who study dinosaurs, that is. Dinosaur bones abound in this dry, stony, barren desert.

A Dinosaur Graveyard

On a sizzling summer day, **paleontologists** made an amazing discovery in the Gobi Desert. The bone hunters fought clouds of stinging, whipping sand. Then they stepped carefully down steep cliffs. But the struggle was worth it. Everywhere they looked, there were bones. One paleontologist found a skeleton of an oviraptor, an **extinct** ostrich-like dinosaur. But that was not all!

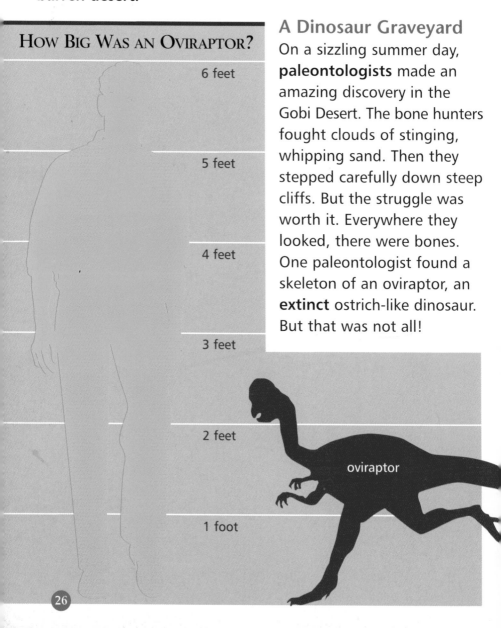

HOW BIG WAS AN OVIRAPTOR?

6 feet

5 feet

4 feet

3 feet

2 feet

1 foot

oviraptor

Relatives of Birds?

The scientist chipped away at the rock surrounding the oviraptor. He couldn't believe his eyes! About 22 huge eggs appeared. Eighty million years ago, this oviraptor had been sitting on a nest of eggs! Before this, no one knew that dinosaurs cared for their young or that the oviraptor had something in common with modern birds. Since that time, many scientists have become even more convinced that dinosaurs are the ancestors of birds.

This illustration shows what scientists think the oviraptor's head looked like.

A scientist is examining one of the fossil dinosaur eggs found in the Gobi Desert.

The Wild Horse of Mongolia

Roam the grasslands and you may find a herd of takhi. Why are these wild horses so special? They nearly became extinct, but they're on the road back!

The Takhi—Not Your Ordinary Horses!

You can't ride the wild takhi or stroke their noses. You can't even get close to them because they are difficult to tame. A closer look through binoculars reveals that they are less than four feet high and are about the size of a Shetland pony. Their necks are much thicker than those of other horses. They're also frisky and tough. In fact, the word takhi means "spirited" in Mongolian.

Unlike tamed horses, the takhi have short-haired manes that don't extend beyond their ears.

Other, tamed horses are vital to the Mongolians' way of life.

The Takhi Make a Comeback

Wild horse lovers are celebrating! About 210 takhi are living freely in Mongolia. So why jump for joy? From 1968–1992, there were none of them in the wild. Fortunately, many takhi were then living in zoos. Without zoos, the little horse would have become extinct.

Returning the takhi to Mongolia has been difficult. Wolves and sub-zero cold have caused some deaths. But the takhi's human friends haven't given up. They have built winter shelters for the horses and have kept watch over them.

Maybe someday you'll visit a unique place like this!

WHO MILKS THE REINDEER?

Imagine that your family herds reindeer. When school is over, you jump onto the back of a friendly young reindeer. You race across the green hills where your neighbors' reindeer are grazing. As the sun sets, you hurry home for a supper of tea with reindeer milk, reindeer cheese, and bread. Be sure to go to bed early! You have to milk the reindeer at dawn.

Fact File

Unique Places, One-of-a-Kind Birds

Bird	Unique Place	Favorite Habitat	Most Unusual Feature
Shag	Iceland	Rocky cliffs, ocean	Baby shags get food by putting their heads into their parents' throats, where there is partly-digested food.
Galapagos Penguins	Galapagos Islands	Rocks by the sea	These penguins love a warm climate.
Lammergeyer	Mongolia	Gobi Desert	This vulture has a wingspan that sometimes reaches 3 yards in length.
Swallow-tailed Gull	Galapagos Islands	Rocks by the sea (rocky shoreline)	This is the only gull in the world that hunts at night.
Whooper Swan	Iceland	Wetlands, lakes, flooded farmlands	These swans make a trumpet-like call that sounds like "whoop-whoop."
Frigate	Galapagos Islands	Bushes and shrubs near the shoreline	To attract a mate, the male frigate puffs up his bright-red throat pouch.
White-tailed Eagle	Iceland	High cliff regions	This bird was hunted to near-extinction but is making a comeback.

Glossary

endangered threatened with becoming extinct

extinct no longer existing

geysers hot springs that gush a fountain of steam and hot water high into the air

glaciers huge sheets of ice that do not disappear in the summer months

habitat the place where an animal or plant is usually found in nature

lava hot liquid rock that pours out of a volcano

manchineel a poisonous tree; tortoises on the Galapagos Islands can eat its leaves, however

magma hot liquid rock beneath the earth's surface

paleontologists scientists who find and study animal fossils

species a group of animals that are like one another; a group of animals that can breed and have offspring

geyser

Index